הַנֵּרוֹת הַלָּלוּ

Haneirot Halalu
These Lights are Holy

a home celebration of
CHANUKA

Edited by Elyse D. Frishman
Illustrated by Leonard Baskin

CCAR
PRESS
The Central Conference of American Rabbis

Copyright © 1989
Central Conference of American Rabbis
192 Lexington Ave., New York, NY 10016

ISBN: 0-88123-006-5

Printed in the United States of America

CENTRAL CONFERENCE OF AMERICAN RABBIS

The Conference is the professional association of Reform rabbis in the United States, Canada and abroad, founded in 1889 by Isaac Mayer Wise. It is the largest publisher of Jewish liturgy in the world. Other related publications include: *Gates of Mitzvah* (1979); *Gates of the Seasons* (1983); *Shabbat Manual* (1972); *Gates of the House* (1977); *The Five Scrolls* (1984) and *A Passover Haggadah* (1974). Write for a complete catalogue.

Acknowledgments

Many colleagues contributed their insights and creative efforts to this liturgical project. There were many possible paradigms for a Chanuka liturgy: we tried several before resolving to use this format. Rabbi Joseph Glaser did the first division of the Chanuka stories into eight thematic, sequential segments, which began to put us on the track toward the existing work. I am grateful for his ongoing support and vision. Dr. Lawrence Hoffman's early work is deeply appreciated as is his personal support in guiding me; he is a mentor of the highest order. As an earlier chair of the Liturgy Committee and as a liturgical editor, he worked with Mr. Moshe Perlman of Israel to formulate early versions of the text for committee consideration. Rabbi Edward Treister made substantial contributions in the initial stage, helping to focus our direction. During this time, Rabbi Jordan Pearlson also gave his important perspective. Rabbi A. Stanley Dreyfus offered ongoing, gentle advice and editorial expertise. Rabbi Herbert Bronstein chaired the Liturgy Committee during the project's development, and was ever-present with sound insights and wisdom. Rabbi Elliot Stevens was meticulous and persistent in his excellent supervision of the production.

Leonard Baskin is an artist of extraordinary dimension and has given us truly beautiful art. The book itself was designed by Mr. Steven Manowitz of Palinurus Productions of New York. We thank the Union of Hebrew American Congregations for permission to use their logo for our Chanuka motif. Mr. Richard Scheuer contributed generously at the inception of the project, which helped to get it under way. We are grateful for his recognition of the need for this liturgy.

Certain people open our eyes to God and inspire us to sing. To my husband, Rabbi Daniel Freelander and my children, Adam Nathan and Jonah Harry, I dedicate this effort. You are the lights that illumine my life; you are the songs that bear these words to God.

> Rabbi Elyse D. Frishman
> Erev Shabbat Bemidbar 5749
> The Reform Temple of Suffern
> Suffern, New York

Introduction

This liturgy was born of a desire to increase the spiritual celebration of Chanuka. It is for families, for adults, for college students, for any Jew seeking to enhance the lighting of the Chanuka menora. Each night offers a retelling of the story, a poetic prayer reading and the Chanuka blessings. Towards the end of the volume, there is a prayer for the Shabbat during Chanuka, and the traditional prayer "Haneirot Halalu." Finally, you will find wonderful traditional and contemporary Chanuka music with notation, a recipe for latkes, and instructions on how to play the dreidel game.

Some Guidance on Usage:

Ideally, one would begin at "the First Day" and read both the story and the prayer before lighting the candles and reciting the blessings. This might be followed by the reading of "Haneirot Halalu" on page 34, and singing songs. On the second evening, one would read from "the Second Day," and so on. However, this book is designed so that each day may stand on its own. If you were to miss an evening, you could pick up again on the next day, without feeling that you had lost the full thread of the story.

This is a volume to grow with. Families with small children might begin with just the story and blessings, or even with just the blessings. The music and activities are age appropriate for everyone.

Readings may be spoken in unison or by one person.

On Lighting the Menora:

One candle is lit for each night. The candle for the first night is placed on the right side of the eight-branched menora (chanukia). On each subsequent night, an additional candle is placed to the left of the preceding night's candle. The lighting proceeds from left to right, so that the new candle is kindled first. Each night, the shamash is lit first, followed by recitation of the first blessing. The other candles are then lit with the shamash, ending with the recitation of the second (and, on the first night, the third) blessings.

עם ההלכים בחשך

ראו אור גדול

No practical use may be made of the Chanuka lights, such as illuminating the room. Therefore, according to Jewish tradition, a special helper candle known as the *shamash* is used to light the others and provide light.

On Friday evening, the Chanuka candles are lit before Shabbat candles; you may choose an additional reading for Shabbat on page 35. On Saturday evening, the candles are lit at Havdala. The kindling of the Chanuka lights in the synagogue is no substitute for kindling them at home.

It is an old custom to place the menora where its lights will be visible from the outside. The public proclamation of the miracle of Chanuka is part of the observance of the holiday. Displaying the menora is a demonstration of our pride and identity.

THE FIRST DAY

Our Story...

In the year 170 BCE, the Syrian-Greek ruler Antiochus took control of the land of the Jews. Antiochus hated our people because we worshipped God instead of him. Our law was Torah, but Antiochus's law was his own. In furious outrage, he overthrew the High Priest in Jerusalem, and plundered the Temple. Jewish priests throughout the country were ordered to abolish the Torah.

In the village of Modin, one priest, Mattathias, held his ground. Brave and proud, he stood against the pagan soldiers and defied their commands. In swift and spontaneous action, his followers rose to battle, and the enemy was overcome.

Thus began the Jewish revolt against the darkness of tyranny.

הָעָם הַהֹלְכִים בַּחֹשֶׁךְ רָאוּ אוֹר גָּדוֹל.

The people who walked in darkness
have seen a great light.

O God,
The hand that lights this candle
Might be a young child in Jerusalem,
       a dreamer in Kiev,
       an American Jew.

Wherever Jews dwell,
We celebrate You, God.

      On this night of dedication,
      We kindle our first flame.
      May this light shine with hope
      For the freedom of all people.

Light the Shamash candle first, then use it to light the other candle.

בָּרוּךְ אַתָּה יְיָ, אֱלֹהֵינוּ מֶלֶךְ הָעוֹלָם, אֲשֶׁר קִדְּשָׁנוּ בְּמִצְוֹתָיו, וְצִוָּנוּ לְהַדְלִיק נֵר שֶׁל חֲנֻכָּה.

Ba-ruch a-ta A-do-nai, E-lo-hei-nu me-lech ha-o-lam, a-sher ki-de-sha-nu be-mits-vo-tav, ve-tsi-va-nu le-had-lik ncir shel Cha-nu-ka.

We praise You, Adonai our God, Ruler of the universe, who hallows us with Your mitzvot and commands us to kindle the Chanuka lights.

בָּרוּךְ אַתָּה יְיָ, אֱלֹהֵינוּ מֶלֶךְ הָעוֹלָם, שֶׁעָשָׂה נִסִּים לַאֲבוֹתֵינוּ בַּיָּמִים הָהֵם בַּזְּמַן הַזֶּה.

Ba-ruch a-ta A-do-nai, E-lo-hei-nu me-lech ha-o-lam, she-a-sa ni-sim la-a-vo-tei-nu ba-ya-mim ha-heim ba-ze-man ha-zeh.

We praise You, Adonai our God, Ruler of the universe, who performed wondrous deeds for our ancestors in days of old, at this season.

On the first night only

בָּרוּךְ אַתָּה יְיָ, אֱלֹהֵינוּ מֶלֶךְ הָעוֹלָם, שֶׁהֶחֱיָנוּ וְקִיְּמָנוּ וְהִגִּיעָנוּ לַזְּמַן הַזֶּה.

Ba-ruch a-ta Λ-do-nai, E-lo-hei-nu me-lech ha-o-lam, she-he-che-ya-nu ve-ki-ye-ma-nu ve-hi-gi-a-nu la-ze-man ha-zeh.

We praise You, Adonai our God, Ruler of the universe, for giving us life, for sustaining us, and for enabling us to reach this season.

For those who recite Haneirot Halalu, the text appears on page 34.

THE SECOND DAY

Our Story...

Despite Mattathias's revolt, the oppression continued.

The hearts of our people wept.
Jerusalem was a city of tears.

Yet, we were taught:
Our faith lends us courage and wisdom.

Legend said that one old man, Eleazar, was brought forth and ordered to break our laws. He thought, "This would lead those younger than me to desert the Teaching. How can I betray the children?"

He was taken prisoner; but he did not give in. The courage of his heart and the wisdom of his soul endured, inspiring others to resist the evils of Antiochus.

Our people continued to fight back with faith in the power of Right overcoming Might.

כִּי נָפַלְתִּי, קָמְתִּי; כִּי־אֵשֵׁב בַּחֹשֶׁךְ, יְהֹוָה אוֹר לִי.

Though I fall, I shall rise; though I sit in darkness,
the Eternal shall be a light to me.

On this night of dedication, we ask:

How was it that Antiochus did not defeat us completely?

Like a happy child who takes a parent for granted,
So we had ignored God.

> Yet, God stayed with us,
> And taught us to live as Jews:
> with love and a law and our land.

"Not for the sake of the place was the people chosen,
But the place for the sake of the people."*

> God, for the sake of Your love,
> Our people fought:
> > not for the shimmer of gold,
> > but for the light of Torah.

As we kindle this menora,
Our eyes open to the light of Your Teaching
And the light of Your love.

*II Maccabees 5:19

*Light the Shamash
candle first, then
use it to light the
other candles.*

בָּרוּךְ אַתָּה יְיָ, אֱלֹהֵינוּ מֶלֶךְ הָעוֹלָם, אֲשֶׁר קִדְּשָׁנוּ
בְּמִצְוֹתָיו, וְצִוָּנוּ לְהַדְלִיק נֵר שֶׁל חֲנֻכָּה.

Ba-ruch a-ta A-do-nai, E-lo-hei-nu me-lech ha-o-lam, a-sher ki-de-sha-nu be-
mits-vo-tav, ve-tsi-va-nu le-had-lik neir shel Cha-nu-ka.

We praise You, Adonai our God, Ruler of the universe, who hallows us
with Your mitzvot and commands us to kindle the Chanuka lights.

בָּרוּךְ אַתָּה יְיָ, אֱלֹהֵינוּ מֶלֶךְ הָעוֹלָם, שֶׁעָשָׂה נִסִּים לַאֲבוֹתֵינוּ
בַּיָּמִים הָהֵם בַּזְּמַן הַזֶּה.

Ba-ruch a-ta A-do-nai, E-lo-hei-nu me-lech ha-o-lam, she-a-sa ni-sim la-a-vo-
tei-nu ba-ya-mim ha-heim ba-ze-man ha-zeh.

We praise You, Adonai our God, Ruler of the universe, who performed
wondrous deeds for our ancestors in days of old, at this season.

For those who recite Haneirot Halalu, the text appears on page 34.

THE THIRD DAY

Our Story...

Throughout the land, tales sprang up about brave Jews. One famous legend described the family of Hannah and her seven children, who were brought before the cruel King Antiochus. He commanded the family to prove their devotion to him by eating foods forbidden by Torah. The oldest child cried, "We love God with all our soul and might!" Enraged, Antiochus slew him on the spot.

The second son was asked, "Will you eat this forbidden food?" This boy, too, defied the king. And so it unfolded, one son after the next, each refusing to obey the wicked king.

Finally, the youngest child stood before Antiochus. He was offered wealth and riches, but he simply shook his head. Loathe to be defeated, the king turned to Hannah. "Convince your son to follow me, and both of you shall live!" Hannah and her son clasped each other's hand and spoke proudly yet softly to Antiochus. "Our love is for each other and our God," they said. And so, the legend says, their lives were taken.

But their faith and courage roused others to action. New battles were fought and won to keep Torah and God and Jews alive.

We have witnessed:
No matter where we dwell in darkness,
The air is bright with God and the light of faith.

כִּי־אַתָּה תָּאִיר נֵרִי; יְהוָֹה אֱלֹהַי יַגִּיהַּ חָשְׁכִּי.

For You light my lamp; the Eternal God
makes bright my darkness.

Like the branches of a menora,
Children reach forth from family.

> From Hannah, her sons drew love and courage.
> She was their teacher, their foundation.
> She was their comfort.
> Her faith sparked theirs.

Family may be near at hand or distant.
But family binds us.
Like the branches of a menora, we grow from a single source.

> And Hannah grasped her children's hands in hers.

Like the branches of a menora, our people rise from God.

> We are Your children.

On this night of dedication, we light candles.

> For family,
> For our people,
> For God.

May these lights remind us to clasp each other's hands.

Light the Shamash candle first, then use it to light the other candles.

בָּרוּךְ אַתָּה יְיָ, אֱלֹהֵינוּ מֶלֶךְ הָעוֹלָם, אֲשֶׁר קִדְּשָׁנוּ בְּמִצְוֹתָיו, וְצִוָּנוּ לְהַדְלִיק נֵר שֶׁל חֲנֻכָּה.

Ba-ruch a-ta A-do-nai, E-lo-hei-nu me-lech ha-o-lam, a-sher ki-de-sha-nu be-mits-vo-tav, ve-tsi-va-nu le-had-lik neir shel Cha-nu-ka.

We praise You, Adonai our God, Ruler of the universe, who hallows us with Your mitzvot and commands us to kindle the Chanuka lights.

בָּרוּךְ אַתָּה יְיָ, אֱלֹהֵינוּ מֶלֶךְ הָעוֹלָם, שֶׁעָשָׂה נִסִּים לַאֲבוֹתֵינוּ בַּיָּמִים הָהֵם בַּזְּמַן הַזֶּה.

Ba-ruch a-ta A-do-nai, E-lo-hei-nu me-lech ha-o-lam, she-a-sa ni-sim la-a-vo-tei-nu ba-ya-mim ha-heim ba-ze-man ha-zeh.

We praise You, Adonai our God, Ruler of the universe, who performed wondrous deeds for our ancestors in days of old, at this season.

For those who recite Haneirot Halalu, the text appears on page 34.

THE FOURTH DAY

Our Story...

Hiding in the mountains, Mattathias and his five sons organized their attacks. One son, Judah Maccabee, emerged as the leader. At night, his bands would swoop down upon unsuspecting enemy troops. Small victories began to grow, and Judah's army gained recruits. One day, he assembled his supporters and called to them:

"Our greatest struggle is at hand. The enemy outnumbers us vastly. But do not fear. They put their trust in weapons and strength; we trust in God. Our faith shall guide us to victory."*

And with visions of the plundered Temple burning in their minds, our soldiers poured out upon the enemy — and won! News of this great event spread throughout the land. And the light of hope was kindled.

*from II Maccabees 8:18

זָרַח בַּחֹשֶׁךְ אוֹר לַיְשָׁרִים; חַנּוּן, וְרַחוּם, וְצַדִּיק.

Light dawns in the darkness for the upright;
for the one who is gracious, compassionate, and just.

Judah's banner waved in the wind, high above,
Calling Jews to gather with pride, to be strong.

The Maccabees had courage and skill.
Ah, so did our enemy.

But our people trusted God,
And the enemy had no faith in God at all.
Thus we overcame them.

Like Moses and Miriam before us,
Overcoming the Egyptians at the Sea,
We danced and sang:

מִי־כָמֹכָה בָּאֵלִם, יְיָ?

Mi cha-mo-cha ba-ei-lim Adonai?
Who is like You, God?

And it is said that from these words,
Judah took his name, Maccabee,
And splashed it across his banner for all to see.

On this night of dedication,
As we kindle these lights,
May our hearts be filled:

We are proud to be Jews.

We thank God for freedom.

Light the Shamash candle first, then use it to light the other candles.

בָּרוּךְ אַתָּה יְיָ, אֱלֹהֵינוּ מֶלֶךְ הָעוֹלָם, אֲשֶׁר קִדְּשָׁנוּ בְּמִצְוֹתָיו, וְצִוָּנוּ לְהַדְלִיק נֵר שֶׁל חֲנֻכָּה.

Ba-ruch a-ta A-do-nai, E-lo-hei-nu me-lech ha-o-lam, a-sher ki-de-sha-nu be-mits-vo-tav, ve-tsi-va-nu le-had-lik neir shel Cha-nu-ka.

We praise You, Adonai our God, Ruler of the universe, who hallows us with Your mitzvot and commands us to kindle the Chanuka lights.

בָּרוּךְ אַתָּה יְיָ, אֱלֹהֵינוּ מֶלֶךְ הָעוֹלָם, שֶׁעָשָׂה נִסִּים לַאֲבוֹתֵינוּ בַּיָּמִים הָהֵם בַּזְּמַן הַזֶּה.

Ba-ruch a-ta A-do-nai, E-lo-hei-nu me-lech ha-o-lam, she-a-sa ni-sim la-a-vo-tei-nu ba-ya-mim ha-heim ba-ze-man ha-zeh.

We praise You, Adonai our God, Ruler of the universe, who performed wondrous deeds for our ancestors in days of old, at this season.

For those who recite Haneirot Halalu, the text appears on page 34.

THE FIFTH DAY

Our Story...

Judah Maccabee and his supporters stood on the hills overlooking Jerusalem. The first battles were over; a calm filled the air.

They entered the city and strode through the marketplace, moving towards the Temple. They pushed from one stall to the next, gaining Jews as they swept through the city.

And then, the Temple stood before them: the sacred site! Our people entered and began to clean away the pagan pollutions. Gently, ardently, they scrubbed and polished until the stones and pillars and altar shone anew.

The Temple stood ready, once again a beacon in the darkness, a light for our people. It was the twenty-fifth of Kislev, exactly three years since the day that Antiochus ruined the Temple.

It was time for the dedication, time to renew the commitment. Our people declared a festival of light for eight days: a celebration of the light of God!

קוּמִי, אוֹרִי, כִּי־בָא אוֹרֵךְ, וּכְבוֹד יְהֹוָה עָלַיִךְ זָרָח.

Arise, shine, for your light has come,
and the splendor of the Eternal shall dawn upon you.

Tonight we recall the task of preparation
When our people purified the Temple.

Judah called, and
Men and women came forth,
Bearing gifts from their hearts.
Each offered a hand in the task of renewal.

Artisans arrived,
Skilled in wood and precious metals.
They re-erected the marble pillars
And gold and silver walls.

All partook in the labor.
Each brought forth an offering.

> But the altar was renewed with love
> From the children of Jerusalem.

This is our offering to You, God:
Our homes, our hearts.
> May our home resemble Yours
> And be filled with love.

God, on this night of dedication,
Reveal Your Presence to us
As we dedicate ourselves to You.

Light the Shamash candle first, then use it to light the other candles.

בָּרוּךְ אַתָּה יְיָ, אֱלֹהֵינוּ מֶלֶךְ הָעוֹלָם, אֲשֶׁר קִדְּשָׁנוּ בְּמִצְוֹתָיו, וְצִוָּנוּ לְהַדְלִיק נֵר שֶׁל חֲנֻכָּה.

Ba-ruch a-ta A-do-nai, E-lo-hei-nu me-lech ha-o-lam, a-sher ki-de-sha-nu be-mits-vo-tav, ve-tsi-va-nu le-had-lik neir shel Cha-nu-ka.

We praise You, Adonai our God, Ruler of the universe, who hallows us with Your mitzvot and commands us to kindle the Chanuka lights.

בָּרוּךְ אַתָּה יְיָ, אֱלֹהֵינוּ מֶלֶךְ הָעוֹלָם, שֶׁעָשָׂה נִסִּים לַאֲבוֹתֵינוּ בַּיָּמִים הָהֵם בַּזְּמַן הַזֶּה.

Ba-ruch a-ta A-do-nai, E-lo-hei-nu me-lech ha-o-lam, she-a-sa ni-sim la-a-vo-tei-nu ba-ya-mim ha-heim ba-ze-man ha-zeh.

We praise You, Adonai our God, Ruler of the universe, who performed wondrous deeds for our ancestors in days of old, at this season.

For those who recite Haneirot Halalu, the text appears on page 34.

THE SIXTH DAY

Our Story...

Our rabbis told this legend: the Temple was covered with filth. There seemed little hope that this ragged band of Jews could rekindle her light, but they began to clean. All traces of false worship were washed away. The menora was polished to a high gleam.

In joy, the people declared, "Let us offer praise to God!" But no oil could be found to light the menora. A great search ensued, and finally, one small container was found. Its oil would last one day, but that would be a splendid day of celebration and rededication to God!

Each branch of the menora was filled with a small amount of oil. Soon, a soft light filled the Temple. The night passed, and then the day... and the light still shone! Another night and day, and then a third; the light would not go out. For eight nights and days, the menora burned steadily, undaunted by that small amount of oil. A miracle! And for each day, our people celebrated a festival of dedication, loving God as God loved them.

A festival of light: Chanuka!

לֹא־יִהְיֶה־לָּךְ עוֹד הַשֶּׁמֶשׁ לְאוֹר יוֹמָם, וּלְנֹגַהּ
הַיָּרֵחַ לֹא־יָאִיר לָךְ; וְהָיָה־לָךְ יְהֹוָה לְאוֹר עוֹלָם,
וֵאלֹהַיִךְ לְתִפְאַרְתֵּךְ.

*No more shall the sun be your light by day, nor shall
the moon give light to you by night; but the Eternal
will be your everlasting light, and your God your glory.*

On this night of dedication,
We recall the legend of the oil.
We kindle these lights for the miracle of faith.

Once, upon a mountain,
Moses stood in awe before a burning bush.

Later, upon the Temple Mount,
Our people beheld the menora.

    Like the burning bush,
    The oil burned unconsumed.

God spoke again through fire:
Your light shall never go out;
My people will always shine.

God, when we feel afraid,
Let us feel your warmth.
Darkness shall never blind us;
The light of faith will be our guide.

Light the Shamash candle first, then use it to light the other candles.

בָּרוּךְ אַתָּה יְיָ, אֱלֹהֵינוּ מֶלֶךְ הָעוֹלָם, אֲשֶׁר קִדְּשָׁנוּ בְּמִצְוֹתָיו, וְצִוָּנוּ לְהַדְלִיק נֵר שֶׁל חֲנֻכָּה.

Ba-ruch a-ta A-do-nai, E-lo-hei-nu me-lech ha-o-lam, a-sher ki-de-sha-nu be-mits-vo-tav, ve-tsi-va-nu le-had-lik neir shel Cha-nu-ka.

We praise You, Adonai our God, Ruler of the universe, who hallows us with Your mitzvot and commands us to kindle the Chanuka lights.

בָּרוּךְ אַתָּה יְיָ, אֱלֹהֵינוּ מֶלֶךְ הָעוֹלָם, שֶׁעָשָׂה נִסִּים לַאֲבוֹתֵינוּ בַּיָּמִים הָהֵם בַּזְּמַן הַזֶּה.

Ba-ruch a-ta A-do-nai, E-lo-hei-nu me-lech ha-o-lam, she-a-sa ni-sim la-a-vo-tei-nu ba-ya-mim ha-heim ba-ze-man ha-zeh.

We praise You, Adonai our God, Ruler of the universe, who performed wondrous deeds for our ancestors in days of old, at this season.

For those who recite Haneirot Halalu, the text appears on page 34.

THE SEVENTH DAY

Our Story...

The Temple was rededicated. But the war was not over. The enemy
gathered its forces for a final battle: tens of thousands of soldiers,
thousands of horses, and the crushing weight of eighty elephants.
Elephants in the land of Israel! The Jews trembled before the news;
how could such a power be defeated?

Judah and his supporters moved nervously towards the enemy camp.
Suddenly, an angel appeared before them, dressed in white,
brandishing a golden weapon. "An angel of God! Our protector!" cried
the Jews. With tears of gratitude, they blessed God for this sign. Their
courage renewed, they came upon the enemy and conquered them.*

The few against the many,
Right versus Might.
The light of God pierces the darkness of evil.

*from II Maccabees 11:8ff

יְהֹוָה אוֹרִי וְיִשְׁעִי; מִמִּי אִירָא?

Adonai is my light and help; whom shall I fear?

On this night of Chanuka, we ask ourselves:
How do we find God?

Our senses bring us wonder
In these special lights:
Their warmth, their glow, the rich flames.

We find God when love fills us
And we give from our hearts,
When, though tempted to do wrong,
We are moved to do right.

We find God through our sense of history,
In the glow of this moment,
And even in the hope of the future.

We find God when we rejoice,
As we do tonight,
With praise and love for life.

Light the Shamash candle first, then use it to light the other candles.

בָּרוּךְ אַתָּה יְיָ, אֱלֹהֵינוּ מֶלֶךְ הָעוֹלָם, אֲשֶׁר קִדְּשָׁנוּ בְּמִצְוֹתָיו, וְצִוָּנוּ לְהַדְלִיק נֵר שֶׁל חֲנֻכָּה.

Ba-ruch a-ta A-do-nai, E-lo-hei-nu me-lech ha-o-lam, a-sher ki-de-sha-nu be-mits-vo-tav, ve-tsi-va-nu le-had-lik neir shel Cha-nu-ka.

We praise You, Adonai our God, Ruler of the universe, who hallows us with Your mitzvot and commands us to kindle the Chanuka lights.

בָּרוּךְ אַתָּה יְיָ, אֱלֹהֵינוּ מֶלֶךְ הָעוֹלָם, שֶׁעָשָׂה נִסִּים לַאֲבוֹתֵינוּ בַּיָּמִים הָהֵם בַּזְּמַן הַזֶּה.

Ba-ruch a-ta A-do-nai, E-lo-hei-nu me-lech ha-o-lam, she-a-sa ni-sim la-a-vo-tei-nu ba-ya-mim ha-heim ba-ze-man ha-zeh.

We praise You, Adonai our God, Ruler of the universe, who performed wondrous deeds for our ancestors in days of old, at this season.

For those who recite Haneirot Halalu, the text appears on page 34.

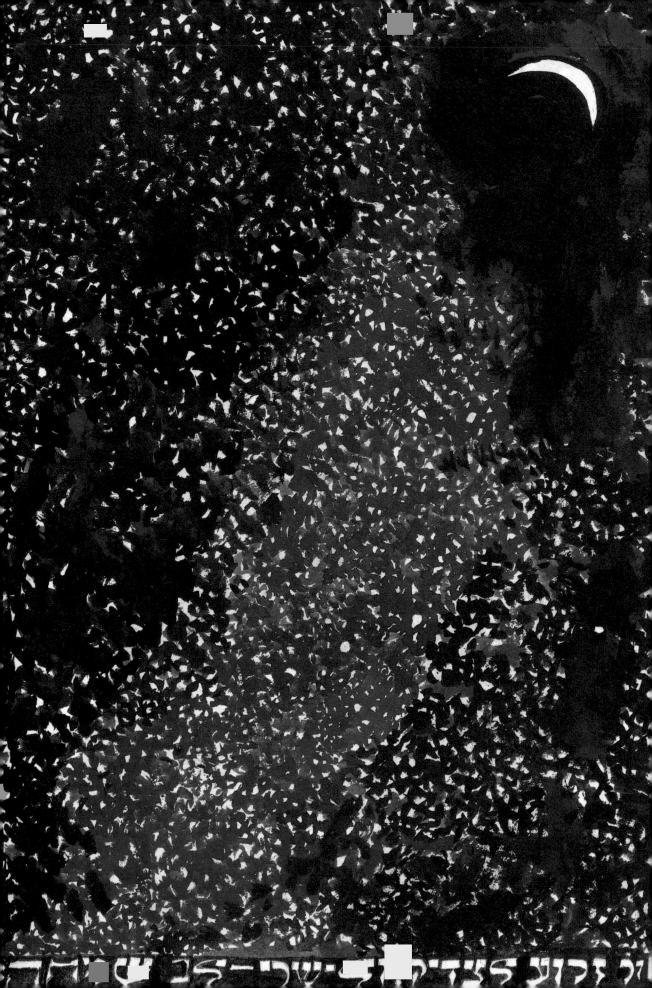

THE EIGHTH DAY

Our Story...

As Chanuka became a fixed observance, the rabbis disagreed about the order of lighting the candles. Shammai argued that all eight lights should be kindled the first night, then decreased one light each night following.

Hillel argued that one light should be kindled the first night, then another be added each night following. "In matters that are sacred," Hillel said, "one should never decrease, but only increase in holy celebration."

Our sages decided according to Hillel. So it is that we begin with one light, and each night add another. On this final night of Chanuka, our entire menora is filled.

The lamps that shined long ago shine anew in our generation. May we, too, live with courage and faith.

כִּי נֵר מִצְוָה, וְתוֹרָה אוֹר.

For the mitzvah is a lamp and the Torah a light.

On this final night of Chanuka,
We recall the very beginning of life,
And we dream about the future.

God's light danced through the universe,
Filling emptiness with being.

God's light bore stars and planets, streaming comets,
milky ways.
Light swept the earth,
The light of life,
The light of God.

Then God's light brought forth Adam,
It nurtured Eve and all their children,
From generation to generation.

So God's light shines in our eyes,
As we kindle the menora.
May our eyes not be dimmed by idols
in our midst.

God, bless us with the light of Your vision
That we might realize peace for all.

Light the Shamash candle first, then use it to light the other candles.

בָּרוּךְ אַתָּה יְיָ, אֱלֹהֵינוּ מֶלֶךְ הָעוֹלָם, אֲשֶׁר קִדְּשָׁנוּ בְּמִצְוֹתָיו, וְצִוָּנוּ לְהַדְלִיק נֵר שֶׁל חֲנֻכָּה.

Ba-ruch a-ta A-do-nai, E-lo-hei-nu me-lech ha-o-lam, a-sher ki-de-sha-nu be-mits-vo-tav, ve-tsi-va-nu le-had-lik neir shel Cha-nu-ka.

We praise You, Adonai our God, Ruler of the universe, who hallows us with Your mitzvot and commands us to kindle the Chanuka lights.

בָּרוּךְ אַתָּה יְיָ, אֱלֹהֵינוּ מֶלֶךְ הָעוֹלָם, שֶׁעָשָׂה נִסִּים לַאֲבוֹתֵינוּ בַּיָּמִים הָהֵם בַּזְּמַן הַזֶּה.

Ba-ruch a-ta A-do-nai, E-lo-hei-nu me-lech ha-o-lam, she-a-sa ni-sim la-a-vo-tei-nu ba-ya-mim ha-heim ba-ze-man ha-zeh.

We praise You, Adonai our God, Ruler of the universe, who performed wondrous deeds for our ancestors in days of old, at this season.

For those who recite Haneirot Halalu, the text appears on page 34.

Haneirot Halalu (These lights are Holy)

In addition to reciting the blessings over kindling the menora, it is traditional to recite these words:

הַנֵּרוֹת הַלָּלוּ אֲנַחְנוּ מַדְלִיקִין עַל הַנִּסִּים וְעַל הַנִּפְלָאוֹת
וְעַל הַתְּשׁוּעוֹת וְעַל הַמִּלְחָמוֹת, שֶׁעָשִׂיתָ לַאֲבוֹתֵינוּ
בַּיָּמִים הָהֵם בַּזְּמַן הַזֶּה.
וְכָל שְׁמֹנַת יְמֵי חֲנֻכָּה הַנֵּרוֹת הַלָּלוּ קֹדֶשׁ הֵם, וְאֵין לָנוּ
רְשׁוּת לְהִשְׁתַּמֵּשׁ בָּהֶם אֶלָּא לִרְאוֹתָם בִּלְבָד, כְּדֵי
לְהוֹדוֹת וּלְהַלֵּל לְשִׁמְךָ הַגָּדוֹל עַל־נִסֶּיךָ וְעַל־נִפְלְאוֹתֶיךָ
וְעַל־יְשׁוּעָתֶךָ.

We kindle these lights because of the wondrous deliverance You performed for our ancestors.

During these eight days of Chanuka, these lights are sacred; we are not to use them but only to behold them, so that their glow may rouse us to give thanks for Your wondrous acts of deliverance.

FOR SHABBAT CHANUKA

*For those nights when Chanuka falls on Shabbat, the following
passage is read after the lighting of the chanukia and the
recitation of the Chanuka blessing:*

A reading based on the Haftara, from the Book of Zechariah 4:1-6.

We recall the vision of Zechariah, the prophet.

An angel touched me, and
I awoke from my sleep.
"What do you see?" she whispered.

I saw a menora all of gold,
With seven branches and seven lamps.

"What more do you see?" she pressed.

And there were two olive trees,
One on each side of the menora.
And coming out from each tree were seven pipes,
Bringing fresh oil to the menora's seven lamps.

And the angel asked, "Do you know what these are for?"
I shook my head.
"This is the symbol of our faith.
The two trees are our leaders:
The ruler and the high priest,
Who nurtured our people with
God's guiding light.
Just as God had charged them:
'Not by might, nor by power, but by My spirit
Shall we all live in peace.'"

The Shabbat candles are then lit.

Tzedeka: Chanuka *gelt* (money) was given traditionally to the poor and to children; the children would use the coins for dreidel games. Students also received *gelt* as a study incentive. We are grateful for so much: our freedom, food and shelter, the breath of life. In preparation for Chanuka, you might create a special Chanuka Tzedeka box; each night of the celebration, before kindling the menora, some coins would be contributed. At the conclusion of Chanuka, the collection would be offered to a special charity of your choosing.

The Game of Dreidel: Long winter nights are brightened with the joy of celebrating Chanuka. The spinning game of dreidel has been popular for centuries. The dreidel (top) has four sides; each side is imprinted with a Hebrew letter. The letters on the dreidel stand for the expression: "Neis gadol haya sham" — "A great miracle happened there." (In Israel, the last letter "Shin" is replaced with a "Pei," to change the phrase to "Neis gadol haya po" — "A great miracle happened here."

Each person begins the game with a supply of counters. Players take turns spinning the dreidel until it lands.

נ	Nun "none" — gets nothing
ג	Gimel "get" — takes entire pot
ה	Hei "half" — takes half the pot
ש	Shin "share" — everyone puts one into the pot

Chanuka Latkes: It is customary to eat food fried in oil to recall the legend of the oil. Most noted among Chanuka delicacies is the latke (potato pancake), followed by the increasingly popular jelly doughnut.

<u>Basic latke recipe:</u>
1 large onion
1/2 cup matza meal
7 medium potatoes
2 eggs
salt and pepper to taste
vegetable oil for frying
apple sauce
sour cream

Grate potatoes. Chop onion. Drain excess liquid from both. Mix all ingredients together. Heat oil in large frying pan. Drop batter by tablespoons into the hot oil and fry over medium heat until crisp and golden on each side. (When batter stops bubbling, the side is ready). Drain on paper towels. Serve with applesauce and sour cream.

CHANUKA SONGS

BIRCHOT CHANUKA
BLESSING OF THE CHANUKA CANDLES

Liturgy

Traditional

Ba - ruch a - ta A - do - nai, E - lo - hei - nu me - lech ha - o - lam,

1. a - sher ki - de - sha - nu be - mits - vo - tav, ve - tsi - va - nu le - had - lik neir shel _____ Cha - nu - ka
2. she - a - sa ni - sim la - vo - tei - nu, ba - ya - mim _____ ha _____ heim ba - ze - man ha - zeh.

Ba - ruch a - ta A - do - nai, E - lo - hei - nu me - lech ha - o - lam, she - he - che - ya nu, ve - ki - ye - ma - nu, ve - hi - gi - a - nu la - ze - man ha - ze.

בָּרוּךְ אַתָּה יְיָ, אֱלֹהֵינוּ מֶלֶךְ הָעוֹלָם, אֲשֶׁר קִדְּשָׁנוּ
בְּמִצְוֹתָיו, וְצִוָּנוּ לְהַדְלִיק נֵר שֶׁל חֲנֻכָּה.

בָּרוּךְ אַתָּה יְיָ, אֱלֹהֵינוּ מֶלֶךְ הָעוֹלָם, שֶׁעָשָׂה נִסִּים לַאֲבוֹתֵינוּ
בַּיָּמִים הָהֵם בַּזְּמַן הַזֶּה.

בָּרוּךְ אַתָּה יְיָ, אֱלֹהֵינוּ מֶלֶךְ הָעוֹלָם, שֶׁהֶחֱיָנוּ וְקִיְּמָנוּ
וְהִגִּיעָנוּ לַזְּמַן הַזֶּה.

YEMEI HACHANUKA
O CHANUKA

English verse: F. Minkoff
Hebrew verse: E. Indelman

Folk Song

Lyrics below the staves:

Line 1 (Cm — Fm — Cm):
Ye - mei ha - cha - nu - ka,___ cha - nu - kat mik - da - shei - nu, Be-
Oy Cha - nu - ka, Oy Cha - nu - ka, a yom - tov a she - ner, A
O Cha - nu - ka, O Cha - nu - ka come light the men - o - ra___

Line 2 (Cm — Fm — Cm):
gil___ u - ve - sim - cha, me - ma - lim et li - bei - nu;
lus - ti - ker, a fre - le - her, ni - to noh a - zoi - ner.
Let's___ have a par - ty, we'll all dance the ho - ra.

Line 3 (Cm — Fm — Cm):
Lai - la va - yom se - vi - vo - nei - nu yi - sov.
Al - le naht in dred ___ leh___ sh'pi in ___ mir,
Gath - er round the ta ___ ble we'll give you a treat,

Line 4 (Cm — G7 — Cm):
Suf - ga - ni - yot no - chal bam la - rov! Ha-
Zu - dik he - se lat - koo, est on a shir. Ge-
Shi - ny tops to play with and pan - cakes to eat. And

Line 5 (Cm — Fm — Cm):
i - ru had li - ku Nei - rot Cha - nu - ka ra - bim!
shvin - der, tsindt kin - der, Dee di - nin - ke lih - te - leh ohn.
while we are play - ing the can - dles are burn - ing___ low;

Line 6 (Cm — Fm — Cm — Fm):
Al ha - ni - sim___ ve - al ha - nif - la - ot___ A-
Zingt "Al Ha - ni - sim", loibt Gott far di ni - sim, Un
One for each night they___ shed a sweet light To re-

Ending — 1. (Cm — Bb7 — Eb — G7) / 2. (Cm — G7 — Cm D.C.):
sher cho - le - lu Ma - ka - bim.   sher cho - le - lu Ma - ka - bim.
kumt gi - her tan - tsn in kohn.   kumt gi - her tan - tsn in kohn.
mind us of days long a - go.   mind us of days long a - go.

MA-OZ TZUR
ROCK OF AGES

arr. H. Fromm
English: M. Jastrow
& G. Gottheil

traditional

Ma - oz tzur ye - shu - a - ti le-cha na - eh le-sha-
Rock of A - ges let our song Praise Your sav - ing___

bei - ach, ti - kon beit le - fi - la - ti
pow - er: You a - mid the rag - ing foes

v-sham to - da ne - za bei - ach. Le-eit ta - chin mat -
were our shel - ter - ing tow - er. Fur - ious they as -

bei - ach mi - tzar ham'-na - bei - ach,
sailed us, But Your arm a - vailed_____ us,

az eg - mor be - shir miz - mor cha - nu - kat ha - miz -
And Your word___ broke their sword when our own strength

bei - ach, bei - ach.
failed___ us, failed___ us.

מָעוֹז צוּר יְשׁוּעָתִי,
לְךָ נָאֶה לְשַׁבֵּחַ;
תִּכּוֹן בֵּית תְּפִלָּתִי,
וְשָׁם תּוֹדָה נְזַבֵּחַ.
לְעֵת תָּכִין מַטְבֵּחַ,
מִצָּר הַמְנַבֵּחַ,
אָז אֶגְמוֹר, בְּשִׁיר מִזְמוֹר,
חֲנֻכַּת הַמִּזְבֵּחַ.

MI YEMALEIL?
WHO CAN RETELL?

Adapted by M. Ravina

English verse: B.M. Edidin

Mi ye-ma-leil ge-vu-rot Yis-ra-eil? O - tan mi yim-neh?
Who can re-tell the__ things that be-fell us? Who can count them?

Hein be-chol dor ya - kum ha-gi-bor go - eil ha - am.
In ev-'ry age, a he - ro or sage came to our aid!

Shema! __ Ba- ya - mim ha - heim ba-ze-man ha - zeh, __
Hark! In days of yore, in Is - rael's an - cient land, Brave

Ma - ka - bi mo-shi - a u - fo - deh,
Mac - ca - be - us led the faith ful band. __ But

U - ve-ya-mei - nu kol am Yis - ra - eil,
now all __ Is - rael must as one a - rise, __ Re -

yit - a - hed ya - kum le - hi - ga - el.
deem it - self thru deed and sac - ri - fice.

מִי יְמַלֵּל גְּבוּרוֹת יִשְׂרָאֵל,
אוֹתָן מִי יִמְנֶה?

הֵן בְּכָל דּוֹר יָקוּם הַגִּבּוֹר,
גּוֹאֵל הָעָם.

שְׁמַע! בַּיָּמִים הָהֵם בַּזְּמַן הַזֶּה
מַכַּבִּי מוֹשִׁיעַ וּפוֹדֶה.
וּבְיָמֵינוּ כָּל עַם יִשְׂרָאֵל
יִתְאַחֵד יָקוּם לְהִגָּאֵל!

I HAVE A LITTLE DREIDEL

I have a lit-tle drei-del I made it out of clay. And
when it's dry and rea-dy then drei-del I shall play. O

Chorus:
drei-del, drei-del, drei-del I made it out of clay. And
when it's dry and rea-dy then drei-del I shall play.

2. It has a lovely body
   With leg so short and thin
   And when it is all tired
   It drops and then I win

3. My dreidel's always playful
   It loves to dance and spin
   A happy game of dreidel
   Come play now let's begin

SEVIVON

Verse:L. Lipnis

Folk Song

Se - vi - von, sov, sov, sov, Cha - nu - ka____ hu chag tov!

Cha - nu - ka hu chag tov! se - vi - von,____ sov, sov, sov.

Chag sim-cha____ hu la - am,____ neis ga-dol ha - ya____ sham!____

Neis ga-dol ha - ya sham!__ chag sim-cha____ hu la - am.

NOT BY MIGHT, NOT BY POWER

Text: Zacharia
Music by Debbie Friedman

With strength

Not _____ by _____ might _____ and _____ not _____ by

pow - er but by spir - it a - lone shall

we all live in peace. _____ The

chil - dren sing, _____ the chil - dren _____

dream and their tears may fall ___ but we'll hear them call ___ and an -

oth - er song will rise. ___ An - oth - er song will ___ rise, an -

oth - er song _____ will rise. _____

Not _____ by ___ might _____ and ___ not _____ by

pow - er but by spir - it a - lone shall

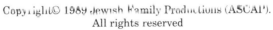

we all live in peace. _____

___ Not by might, _____ not by pow-er _____

___ sha - lom. _____

LIGHT ONE CANDLE

Words and music by
Peter Yarrow

Light one can-dle for the Mac-ca-bee chil-dren. Give
Light one can-dle for the strength that we need to

thanks that their light did-n't die. Light one can-dle for the
nev - er be-come our own foe. Light one can-dle for____

pain they en-dured____ when their right to ex - ist was de - nied.
those who are suf-fering the____ pain we learned so long a - go.

Light one can-dle for the ter - ri - ble sac - ri - fice____
Light one can-dle for the all we be-lieve____ in,____ let

jus - tice and free-dom de - mand. Light one can-dle for the
an - ger not tear us a - part. Light one can-dle____ to

wis-dom to know____ when the peace-mak-er's time is at hand.____
bind us to-geth - er with peace as the song in our heart.____

Don't let the light go out. It's last-ed for so man-y years. Don't let the light go out. Let it shine through our hopes and our fears. Don't let the light go out. Don't let the light go out. Don't let the light go out.

CHANUKA

Verse: L. Kipnis

Folk Song

Cha - nu - ka, Cha - nu - ka, chag ya - feh kol kach,

Or cha - viv mi - sav - viv, gil le - ye - led rach.

Cha - nu - ka, Cha - nu - ka, se - vi - von sov, sov,

Sov, sov, sov, sov, sov, sov, ma na - im va - tov.